Fire Trucks
on the Go

by Beth Bence Reinke

BUMBA BOOKS™

LERNER PUBLICATIONS ◆ MINNEAPOLIS

Note to Educators:

Throughout this book, you'll find critical thinking questions. These can be used to engage young readers in thinking critically about the topic and in using the text and photos to do so.

Lerner Publications Company
A division of Lerner Publishing Group, Inc.
241 First Avenue North
Minneapolis, MN 55401 USA

For reading levels and more information, look up this title at www.lernerbooks.com.

Library of Congress Cataloging-in-Publication Data

The Cataloging-in-Publication Data for *Fire Trucks on the Go* is on file at the Library of Congress.
978-1-5124-8255-3 (lib. bdg.)
978-1-5415-1112-5 (pbk.)
978-1-5124-8256-0 (EB pdf)

Manufactured in the United States of America
1 – CG – 12/31/17

Expand learning beyond the printed book. Download free, complementary educational resources for this book from our website, www.lerneresource.com.

Table of Contents

Fire Trucks

Fire trucks are

important vehicles.

They help put out fires.

There are many types

of fire trucks.

A fire truck rushes to a fire.

Firefighters ride in the

big cab.

One firefighter drives

the truck.

Why do fire trucks need to rush to a fire?

The truck's lights flash.

Sirens blare.

The horn honks.

These signs warn cars to

move out of the way.

Some fire trucks have

a pump.

They get water from

a fire hydrant.

The truck pumps water into

a long hose.

More than one firefighter holds the hose.

They aim at the burning building.

Water sprays on the fire.

Why do you think more than one firefighter holds the hose?

Sometimes there is no fire hydrant.

A tanker truck comes.

It brings water to fight the fire.

What areas might not have fire hydrants?

A ladder truck has a ladder

on top.

The ladder slides out.

It goes way up.

Firefighters climb the ladder.

It helps them reach fires and people

in tall buildings.

19

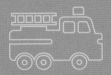

Fire trucks and firefighters help

keep us safe.

Have you ever seen a fire truck?

Parts of a Fire Truck

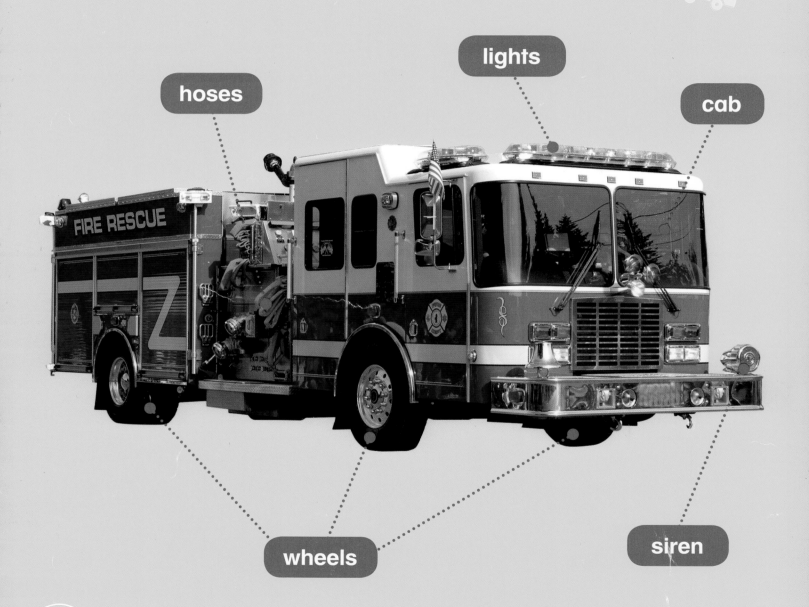

hoses

lights

cab

wheels

siren

Picture Glossary

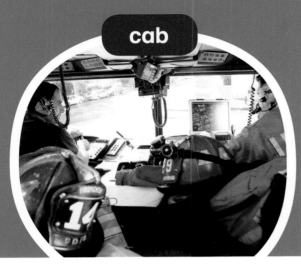

cab

the part of a fire truck where the driver and other firefighters sit

hose

a long tube that carries and sprays water

hydrant

a pipe with a spout to draw water from

sirens

devices that make loud sounds

Read More

Bowman, Chris. *Fire Trucks.* Minneapolis: Bellwether Media, 2017.

Kenan, Tessa. *Hooray for Firefighters!* Minneapolis: Lerner Publications, 2017.

Silverman, Buffy. *How Do Fire Trucks Work?* Minneapolis: Lerner Publications, 2016.

Index

Photo Credits

The images in this book are used with the permission of: © GaryTalton/iStock.com, pp. 4–5; © Monkey Business Images/Shutterstock.com, pp. 6–7, 23 (top left); © slobo/iStock.com, pp. 8–9, 23 (bottom right); © Suzanne Tucker/Shutterstock.com, pp. 10–11, 23 (bottom left); © Dale Stagg/Shutterstock.com, pp. 13, 23 (top right); © Keith Bell/Shutterstock.com, pp. 14–15; © Keith Muratori/Shutterstock.com, pp. 16–17; © ollo/iStock.com, p. 19; © FrankvandenBergh/iStock.com, p. 20; © Le Do/Shutterstock.com, p. 22.

Front Cover: © ryasick/iStock.com.